managing and resolving conflict

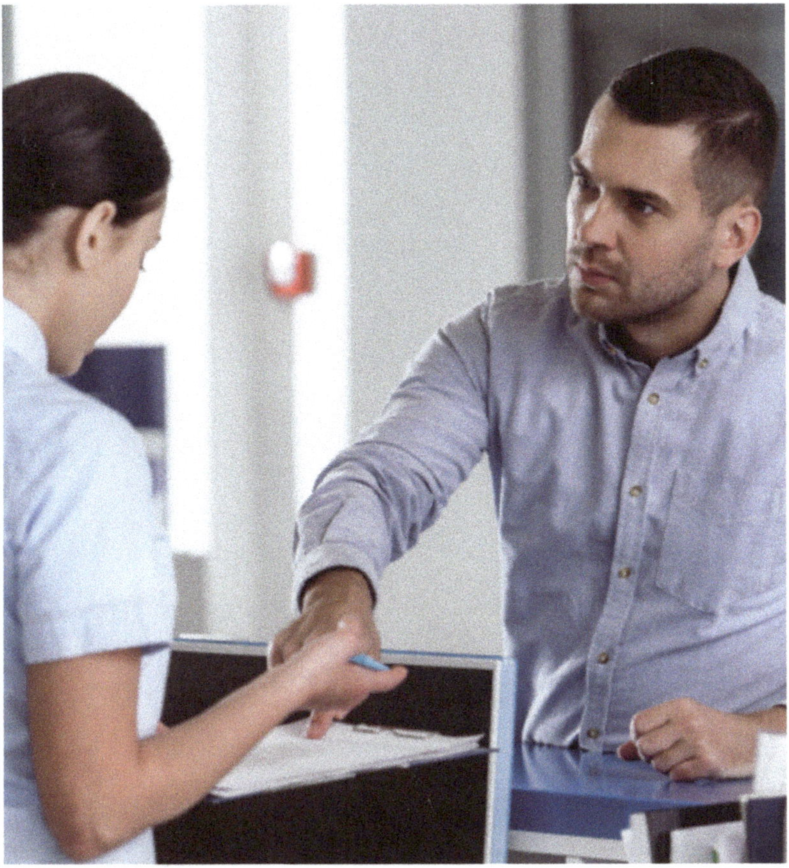

Advice for staff on dealing with disruptive or difficult people

SecuriCare International Limited

Martin House, Barley Rise, Strensall, York, England, YO32 5AA.
Telephone: +44 (0) 1904 492 442
Email: trainers@securicare.com
Website: www.securicare.com

ISBN: 978-0-9560159-6-9

Printed by Wood Richardson Ltd, Digital and Litho Printers,
Royden House, 156 Haxby Road, York, England, YO31 8EY

Copyright 2021. SecuriCare International limited.

All rights reserved. No part of this publication may be reproduced, stored in a retrieval system or transmitted in any form or by any means, electronic, mechanical, photocopying, recording, or otherwise, without prior permission of SecuriCare International Ltd.

Although great care has been taken in the production of this guidance to ensure accuracy, the Publishers cannot under any circumstances accept responsibility for errors, omissions or advice given in this publication.

managing and resolving conflict

Authors
Philip N Hardy
Trevor Platt

Published by
SecuriCare International Ltd

CONTENTS:

Introduction
Definition of Work-Related Violence
Employers Responsibilities
Preventing and Managing Work-Related Violence
Dynamic Risk Assessment
Understanding and Preventing Conflict
Understanding the Causes of Changes in Behaviour
Communication Skills
Incident Management
The Use of Force
Post-Incident

Introduction

Workers who meet or interact with customers and/or the public can face a risk of harm from workplace hazards due to the nature of their work. These hazards can include verbal and physical threats, even violence.

This book is designed to help workers and employers risk assess working conditions and situations that may be encountered and try to provide the safest possible working environment.

The information, guidance and support herein are supplied to ensure those working with customers and/or the public are best prepared to deal with disruptive or difficult people professionally and safely.

Definition of Work-Related Violence

The Health & Safety Executive recognise that employees may have to interact and deal with people who are challenging, threatening and even violent.

> The Health and Safety Executive (HSE) definition of work-related violence is:
>
> *"Any incident in which a person is abused, threatened or assaulted in circumstances relating to their work, involving an explicit or implicit challenge to their safety, well-being or health".*

Employers Responsibilities

Employers have a legal duty towards workers under:
- The Health & Safety at Work Act
- The Management of Health & Safety Regulations

Employers must assess and control the risks in the workplace. They must identify what might cause harm to people and ensure they are doing enough to prevent harm. If they employ more than five workers this must be in the form of a written statement/policy. This should include the following:
- The hazard: what are the things that may cause harm?
- How these things may harm people, e.g., physically, mentally, emotionally
- What is being done to control these risks, e.g., training, personal alarms, tracking devices
- A process for regularly reviewing this assessment

Risk Assessment and Control Measures

Whether conducted as a separate risk assessment or included in general risk assessments, employers must take steps to control risks where necessary. This must include:
- Consultation with those required to work with disruptive/difficult people to identify risks and the required control measures
- Implementing guidance, instructions, training and supervision

- Taking steps to remove risk where possible
- Review risk assessments periodically and update any significant changes

The People
Employers must take into consideration any possible impact on the risk posed by the worker or other people who may be involved during the fulfilment of the work:
- How experienced is the worker?
- Have they received training?
- Is there anything that makes them more vulnerable? Are they young, pregnant, disabled, or inexperienced?
- Who are they expected to engage with and does this increase the risk?

The Environment
Is there anything relating to the environment or venue that impacts the risk?
- How will the worker get to the venue and are there any risks associated with travelling to and from there?
- Are there any heightened risks associated with the venue? E.g., high crime rate, previous incidents or poor design
- Is the venue isolated or difficult to access?

Equipment
They must consider if the safety of the worker would be improved or compromised by the addition or absence of specific equipment:
- Does the worker need/have adequate and reliable means of communication?
- Is there an effective method of calling for help or assistance?
- Is PPE needed? E.g., protective clothing/gloves, body-cam, personal alarm, stab/slash-proof vest

Task or Role
Could the job role or the task increase the risk?
- Are rules or sanctions to be enforced/imposed?
- Are there any cash transactions involved?
- Is it necessary to remove/restrict access to goods or property?
- Will there be a need to deliver a negative or distressing message?

Preventing and Managing Work-Related Violence

Any form of abuse or violence against workers is unacceptable and could seriously affect their psychological and physical health. Training in conflict management and personal safety will help workers recognise potential risks and help them take appropriate action to eliminate or reduce these risks.

Dynamic Risk Assessment

We all risk assess consciously or subconsciously as we go about our lives and make decisions based on our instincts, fears or analysis of the things happening around us.

P - People
Does the behaviour of this person, their associates or bystanders give cause for concern? Do they appear agitated or angry; are they suffering from the effects of alcohol or drugs?

I - Items
Are there any items/objects to hand that could be used as a weapon or to threaten?

E - Environment
Does anything else nearby present a hazard? Be aware of the location; is it isolated or can the exit be blocked? Are there other people around who could assist or call for help? Does the time of day increase the risk?

R - Resources
What resources or support are available? Can we contact someone if we need to? Is there an alternative way of raising the alarm? If needed, is there anything we can use to help protect ourselves?

Is it safe to carry on with the task/interaction or should we move away or leave the area?

Understanding and Preventing Conflict

The best way to deal with difficult, angry or aggressive individuals is to make a positive interaction/intervention as early as possible. The earlier we deal with the underlying problem, concern or frustration, the less chance there is of the behaviour escalating. To effectively manage difficult people, it is important to explore and understand the causes and functions of behaviour.

To understand how situations develop, let's take a closer look at what influences people's moods or feelings.

What a person thinks about the situation will affect how they feel, and if they feel strongly enough about the situation, this change in their emotional state can lead to a change in how they behave towards others. Their attitude and behaviour will in turn influence how others act and behave towards them; this is referred to as the Betari Box Theory and the following diagram is sometimes called the Betaris Box.

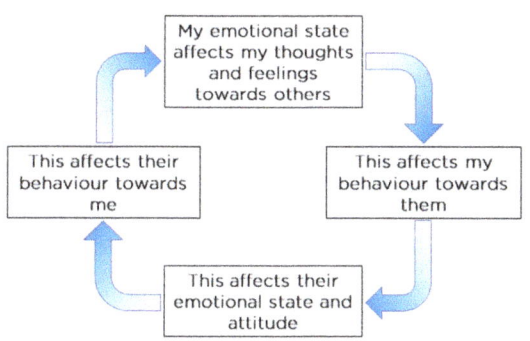

By positively changing our behaviour and attitude the behaviour of others will naturally change as well.

In short, our feelings and attitude will directly influence our behaviour towards others, and this will affect how they feel and behave towards us.

This emphasises the need to interact in a positive way.

Understanding the Causes of Changes in Behaviour

There will always be people who are difficult to interact with, but the majority of people are quite reasonable and only express negative feelings and behaviour when they feel upset, aggrieved, or frustrated by their circumstances, or someone else's attitude or actions.

How a person feels and responds to their circumstances can be the result of experiences and events that take place over hours, days, weeks, months, or even years. We are not usually in a position to help with the long-term influences affecting their current emotional or mental state, we can, however, help them through their current circumstances and/or issue. If we engage with the person with an empathic approach based on the assumption that their behaviour is only happening for a reason, we are much more likely to have a positive interaction.

The following Iceberg Theory illustrates how long, medium, and short-term influences all contribute to a person reaching a crisis point. Most of these influences are unknown or are not visible to us, but by recognising when a person has reached a crisis point, our next interaction could determine whether or not their behaviour escalates or de-escalates.

Iceberg Theory

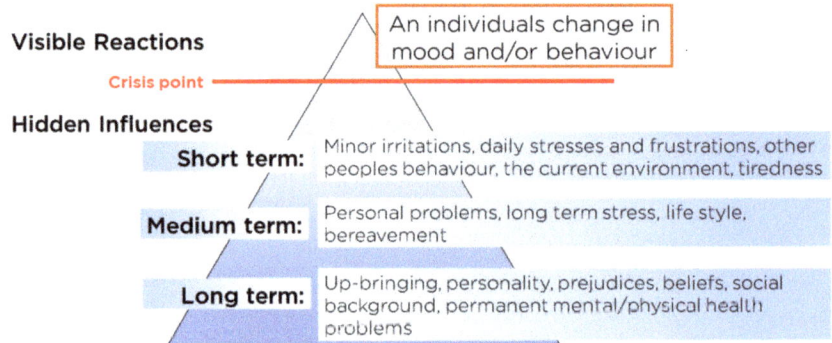

Patterns of Behaviour

There are some people who can go from calm to violent in a very short period; thankfully very few people fit this profile and most people follow a similar pattern of escalation as their feelings and behaviour change.

When people are in a state of calm we normally find them easy to get on with, which makes communication easier. When someone is frustrated, distressed or angry, however, we need to think carefully about how we communicate with them. Events beyond our control may cause people's behaviour to escalate; this might mean the person is agitated before we meet them.

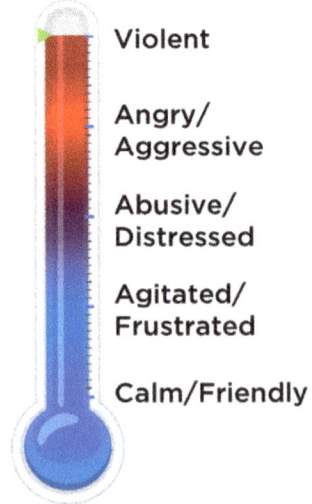

Most people's behaviour will not escalate any further than the angry stage, because of their ability to manage and regulate their behaviour, or because of the possible consequences that might arise if they allow their behaviour to escalate any further. It is therefore important to be able to recognise the changes in a person's mood or behaviour when their feelings are expressed negatively.

Having identified that a person is unhappy or angry, an early, positive interaction/intervention will make it easier to control events and de-escalate the situation. Remember, a person who has become angry and abusive may take some time to return to a state of calm, so any further interaction/intervention will need to be carefully managed.

We should try to ensure that we do not expect and therefore invite negative behaviour.

We should always try to:
- Be non-judgemental and do not make assumptions about people just because of how they look or behave
- Remember, behaviour always happens for a reason; try to understand why the person is behaving as they are
- Believe that a positive outcome is possible
- Accept that mistakes can and do happen and that the person may have a genuine reason for being upset or angry
- Look for ways to rectify things in a positive way

Most incidents will be resolved amicably and by communicating effectively with the person.

Communication Skills

Communicating with others is a skill that most of us use every day. Some people are better communicators than others, but the majority of us get it right most of the time. When communication fails people get confused, upset, frustrated, or even angry.

Communication can be described as "the sharing of information" or "the imparting of a message" involving both a transmitter (the person sending the message) and a receiver (the person receiving the message).

How We Communicate

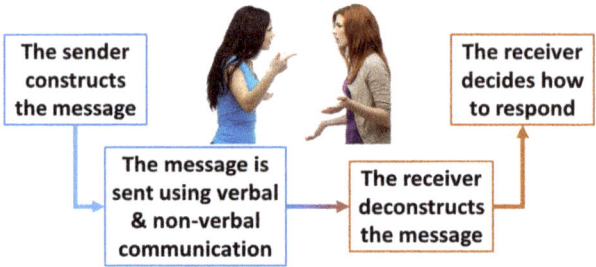

It's not what you say but HOW you say it!

Both the person "transmitting the message" and the person "receiving the message" will be subconsciously influenced by the others non-verbal communication as well as the content of the verbal message.

According to the British Journal of Social and Clinical Psychology, the messages we send are comprised of three parts: words, tone of voice, and body language.

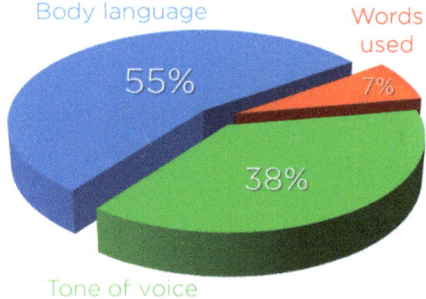

This chart displays the influence that each of these parts plays in the communication process. This demonstrates that 93 % of the messages we transmit or receive is made up of body language and tone of voice. People will determine our true feelings towards them from how we appear and our tone of voice more than the actual words we speak.

Source: British Journal of Clinical and Social Psychology

Body language or non-verbal communication includes:
- Facial expressions
- Eye contact
- Posture or stance
- Positioning of hands
- Personal space (proximity)
- Clothing or appearance
- Touch
- Gestures

When interacting with other people we need to consider the effect that our body language and our presence is having. When speaking, we must control our tone of voice and avoid raising our voice, shouting, or talking too quickly.

Barriers to Communication

We may sometimes come up against barriers to communication; factors that the environment or individuals bring to the situation that have an impact on the communication process. Even good communication can be disrupted or blocked by potential barriers.

Barriers to communication fall into three main categories:

Environmental Barriers:
The setting within which the conversation is taking place can affect how successful the communication process is. Environmental barriers include:
- The distance between the people trying to communicate
- Any physical barrier such as a screen or partition
- Lots of people talking at the same time
- The level of activity happening whilst we are trying to communicate
- Background noise/sounds
- Distractions
- Lighting

Personal Barriers:
Interpersonal and intrapersonal barriers refer to the human factors that could create a barrier to effective communication.

Interpersonal communication is between two or more people and relates to how well we communicate with others. It includes both verbal and non-verbal communication. It also involves listening and understanding the other person's perspective, how well we can problem solve and negotiate, and our ability to be assertive and make decisions.

Intrapersonal communication is between you and yourself and relates to emotional intelligence. It includes self-confidence and discipline, our self-awareness and how we conceive ourselves, our ability to concentrate and focus and overcome distractions.

Cultural Barriers:
Culture can be defined as "a particular social group or organisation characterised by a defined look, mindset, attitude or behaviour". Cultural groups can be organised on the grounds of:
- Age
- Education
- Social status
- Race
- Religion
- Political beliefs
- Personal values
- Gender
- Economic position
- Health
- Beauty
- Popularity

Overcoming Barriers to Communication

The first step to overcoming barriers to communication is to ensure that we don't introduce any barriers ourselves. The following steps are offered as a way of optimising the communication process.

Overcoming Barriers to Communication

- ✓ Listening
- ✓ Asking Questions
- ✓ Clarifying
- ✓ Summarising

Listening:
Active Listening involves more than just hearing the words a person is saying, it's also about being able to understand what the person means. Not only do we need to listen, but we also need to be able to convince the other person that we are listening and understand what they are saying. A person is less likely to complain if we can demonstrate that we are listening, are interested in what they have to say, and they believe we are trying to help.

We need to allow the person time to explain their point of view without interrupting them, even if we don't agree with what they are saying. Often people simply need to talk to someone to help them release some internal frustration or anger. We should always focus on what they say, rather than how it makes us feel.

Asking Questions:
There are two types of questions that we can use: **Open** and **Closed**.

Open questions invite the person to communicate freely, allowing them to express themselves and allowing them to release any internal frustrations or anger. They ask the person to think and reflect, give their opinions and express their feelings.

Closed questions can be used to restrict the person's responses by limiting them to a simple "yes" or "no" answer, which can help us to control the tone and direction of the conversation. Closed questions allow us more time to speak and explain things in a calm, positive, and helpful manner.

Clarifying:
Using clarifying statements is a way of ensuring that everyone involved in the conversation understands the issues and the possible outcomes. They allow us to demonstrate that we have listened and can offer a solution.

Summarising:
To conclude a conversation, we can summarise what has been discussed and the possible solutions, options, or outcomes available.

Despite our best efforts, there are times when these techniques fail to prevent the situation from escalating to a more hazardous level. However, by attempting to communicate, by listening, and by demonstrating a willingness to help, our interaction should be seen as a positive one, which will if nothing else, promote positive witnessing.

Incident Management

There are common warning signs that a person is becoming agitated or angry, such as arguing or raising their voice, staring, suddenly standing, invading personal space, or pushing and shoving. We also need to be aware of any sudden changes in mood or lack of responses to questions; sometimes a person may just go quiet or stop communicating.

We need to follow our instincts; if the situation or the person(s) involved are creating an unsafe environment we need to consider leaving the area. Where there is a risk of physical violence, personal safety becomes the overriding priority.

Dealing with a high-stress situation involving aggressive, threatening or violent behaviours will have an additional impact on everyone involved.

Managing the Fight or Flight Response

When faced with angry or threatening behaviour, or asked to do something we may not be comfortable doing, we usually experience the effects of stress to some degree. The human body's natural response to stress is to either fight the threat or run away from it, hence the term "Fight or Flight".

The stress response is a primitive survival response that prepares us to act decisively to any developing danger or immediate perceived threat. It is a normal and natural response and can occur to differing degrees of intensity depending upon the situation and our past experiences. Although most of us rarely experience life-threatening situations in modern life, this primitive survival response still occurs when we perceive we are in danger or when we are being threatened.

The Effects of Stress

The symptoms of stress can be many and varied and they can affect people in many different ways. Some of the more common effects include:

Visible effects:
- Agitation
- Difficulty speaking
- Muscular tension
- Sweating
- Breathing faster
- Pupils dilate
- Shaking
- Red-faced

Hidden effects:
- Adrenaline rush
- Blood is diverted away from the digestive system, causing feelings of nausea or sickness
- Dry mouth
- Loss or reduction of peripheral vision
- Heart rate increases
- Thinking becomes difficult or focused on the threat

Experiencing stress symptoms is not a sign of failure or an indication that we are not capable of performing our job, it is simply an indicator that we are dealing with a challenging or stressful situation and our body is registering and responding to this.

These changes are caused, in part, by the release of **adrenaline** into the bloodstream. One crucial effect this has is on our ability to reason with common sense. The brain finds it harder to control rational thought and is more prone to instinctive responses.

The key is to try to stay or at least appear, *calm*. The following techniques can be used to help manage the stress response.

Anticipate Difficulties:
With training and experience, we can learn to anticipate some of the difficulties and challenges that we could face and therefore be better prepared in the event of them occurring.

Controlled Breathing:
By taking a deep breath and breathing out slowly, we can reduce stress in two ways:
- It supplies the brain with more oxygen to help optimise thinking capacity
- The regulation of the breathing process will help to facilitate relaxation

Try to Relax Muscular Tension:
Muscular tension can promote negative thinking, which can result in the sustained release of stress hormones. By relaxing and loosening muscle tension we:
- Become more relaxed physically, which will help us to think more clearly
- Our body language will become more relaxed. This will mean the non-verbal signals we are sending out will be more conducive to calming and de-escalation

Mental Distance:
It is easy to become personally and emotionally involved in an incident, especially if the abuse or threats are directed towards us. We should:
- Try to keep a "mental distance" by focusing on the situation and solutions and not the behaviour and the people involved
- Remember, despite what they may be saying, we are probably not the cause of the person's change in mood or behaviour

De-Escalation

De-escalation can be looked at in three phases, the **Calming Phase**, **Building Rapport**, and **Reaching a Positive Conclusion**.

Calming Phase:
To begin to de-escalate a difficult situation we must first instil an element of calm.

We can do this by allowing the person time or space and by moving away if necessary.

Adopt a relaxed and open posture by standing slightly to one side, at 45°. Our hands should be kept open and between us and the person. When talking remember to maintain an even tone and pitch and speak slowly.

When we have demonstrated our ability to stay calm, and have calmed the person down, we can begin to build a rapport with them.

Building Rapport:
Using the techniques discussed in Communication Skills can help us to build a rapport with the person. Remember, sometimes people have a genuine reason for being frustrated and angry and just need to have someone listen, empathise and offer help.

Reaching a Positive Conclusion:
Reaching a positive conclusion can sometimes just mean that we have not made a situation any worse. Hopefully, the majority of incidents will end positively. To help this process we should be clear when someone's behaviour is unacceptable. State what is achievable to help maintain realistic expectations. This may help them re-evaluate their position and look for an amicable solution rather than continue to lead the situation to a negative conclusion.

The Use of Force

In some unfortunate circumstances, we may have to use physical force to leave an incident/location or to protect ourselves; it is important to remember that the action taken will be judged on the following basis:

"was the action taken reasonable and necessary in all the circumstances?"

Section 3 Criminal Law Act 1967 states that:
"A person may use such force as is reasonable in the circumstances"

What is Reasonable and Necessary?

The use of force is only ever reasonable and necessary if all other non-physical strategies have been exhausted or discounted.

Non-physical strategies may include:
- Asking the person to stop what they are doing
- Trying to resolve any conflict
- Removing or reducing any source of frustration
- Taking evasive action such as moving away/leaving

The use of force may be justified if it is being used:
- When acting to save a life or protect an individual from harm or danger
- When acting in self-defence
- To prevent a crime
- To protect property

There are a variety of reasons why force must only be used as a last resort, including:
- Its use can create an increased risk of harm and injury to all those involved
- It increases the risk of allegations
- It could lead to legal action

Was the Force Used Proportionate to the Harm to be Avoided?

The amount or degree of force required will depend on several factors, including:
- The size or strength differences between the people involved
- The number of people who are involved
- The presence of any weapons
- A direct or explicit threat to cause immediate harm
- An increase in the resistance or violence used

Remember, even in the most difficult circumstances there are other options and actions available:
1. **Communication**: continue to try to communicate safely with the person
2. **Attracting attention**: attempt to raise the alarm without increasing the risk
3. **Compliance**: allow the situation to continue until a better opportunity arises, provided there is no immediate risk of harm
4. **Self-defence**: take the actions necessary to protect oneself from harm

Post-Incident

Immediately after an incident, it is important to manage any post-incident requirements.
To do this we may need to do some or all of the following:
- Attend to any first aid concerns; where necessary seek medical assistance
- Comfort/reassure anyone who may have been or still are, affected by the incident
- As we start to calm after the incident the body will release noradrenaline, which will begin to counteract the effects of adrenaline; this can result in headaches, exhaustion, nausea, and possibly symptoms of shock for all those involved in the incident and those who witnessed it
- Provide as much information as possible by completing post-incident report forms or police statements as required
- Collect/preserve any physical evidence

Personal Recovery

Following involvement in a high-stress situation, we may need time to return to our usual state of calm; this process can take longer for some and may involve a range of support measures. There is a practical, moral and legal requirement for employers to ensure that post-incident procedures are available and accessible.
Available support can include:
- A debrief to discuss the incident, including what went well and what didn't but avoid discussing blame or criticising
- Time off or temporary change of responsibilities
- Professional counselling

Reflective Practice

To prevent similar incidents from occurring in the future, we need to learn from past experiences; this will assist in implementing measures and training to eliminate the causes or triggers to these events, or to help staff respond more effectively when this kind of incident reoccurs.

There are various reflective models available, we can use elements of these models to learn from incidents of challenging or hazardous behaviour. Here are the key points:

1 **What happened and why**:
- Describe the incident in a chronological sequence
- Identify what happened before the incident occurred
- Who was involved?
- What specifically, if anything, caused the incident?
- Where did it occur?
- Where time did it occur?
- Were there any other contributing factors?

2 **Analysis**:
- What was your involvement or experience?
- What did others do or experience?
- What went well?
- What did not go well?
- What could have been done differently?
- Do we need to change or amend the way things are done?

3 **Actions**:
- Identify any additional training needs
- Make necessary changes to policy or working practices
- Review or introduce restrictions or penalties

4 **Evaluate**:
- Have the actions taken made a difference?
- Have incidents been reduced or eliminated?
- Do we feel safer and more capable?

Reflection can be a difficult process and some may find it uncomfortable, even distressing. The process should be focused on creating opportunities to prevent incidents from reoccurring, help manage them better when they do reoccur, or change what we do or how we do it to help keep everyone safe.

Summary

People who present behaviours that are challenging, threatening or hazardous can be encountered anywhere and can be from any social, ethnic or economic group.

Legislation and penalties exist to deter most people from becoming aggressive or worse, however, a minority can go too far and create situations that may require us to make difficult decisions and sometimes put ourselves at risk.

We hope the knowledge and advice offered in this book will help and support people who work and interact with difficult and aggressive people more effectively and help keep everyone safe.

Notes

www.ingramcontent.com/pod-product-compliance
Lightning Source LLC
Chambersburg PA
CBHW062115290426
44110CB00023B/2818